I0441181

Sex Offender Resource Guide

Keith Roys

ISBN-13: 978-1505479799
ISBN-10: 1505479797

First Edition

Dedication

This book covers a topic not widely acknowledged and usually ignored or viewed with stereotypical disgust or shame. While some sex offenders refuse to accept responsibility for their past actions and do repeat their crimes, the vast majority of sex offenders willingly accept responsibility for their actions and are seeking not only to change their thoughts, words, and actions, they are struggling to find acceptance in society. This resource guide is an attempt to provide some basic helpful information both for the sex offender and for the public at large. It is therefore dedicated to those who are genuinely repentant and remorseful and are praying to find God's peace in their lives and the opportunity to grow and thrive as contributing members of society.

KEITH ROYS

TABLE OF CONTENTS

KEITH ROYS

Acknowledgements and Warnings

Throughout this book, for ease of writing and reading, the masculine pronouns will be used but it is acknowledged that there are female sex offenders too. This book is intended to be of help to all offenders.

This book is also written from a Christian perspective. God is a forgiving and loving God and His love does heal wounds. His offer of salvation was made to ALL who believe and His forgiveness is 100% available to you (see Chapter 11).

There is some explicit information contained in this book. This was done intentionally. There is no value in trying to sugar coat or downplay events and descriptions. This is not meant to degrade anyone or to stimulate anyone. This is meant to be an honest and candid discussion and to encourage all those involved to be open about what has happened and is happening.

Many good people have contributed to the content of this book. Some are sex offenders, some are their friends and family, some are therapists trained in counseling sex offenders, some are ministers, and some are Parole and Probation officers specializing in supervising sex offenders. Their candid input is greatly appreciated!

Specific thanks to the following:
Debbie, John, Carl, Bill, Tammy, Christine, Scott, Mike, Brian, Cat, Curtis, Kishawn, Tricia, Dan, Chris, Vicki, Jeff, Aaron, and Erin.

1 - Accepting Responsibility

This chapter deals with the critical need for you, the sex offender, to come to terms mentally with your actions and the decisions, or lack thereof, which lead to the offense(s).

It does not matter whether you were a peeping tom or a cold hearted rapist. You may have molested someone, attacked someone, or even killed someone. It may have been a one-time event or it could have been multiple offenses over time. Regardless, you were arrested and you were either convicted or accepted a plea deal. You probably did some time, maybe a lot of time. You may even be serving a life sentence.

This book is not for those sex offenders who refuse to change, who refuse to realize they need help, and who intend to continue to commit sex offenses. Thankfully, that is a very small percentage of the total number of convicted sex offenders.

The majority of sex offenders, once released and in counseling, initially struggle with accepting responsibility for their actions. Outright denial is not uncommon as is blaming others, circumstances, drugs, or alcohol as the reason for their actions that led to their arrest.

You need to really be honest with yourself. NO ONE but you is responsible for what you did. No matter if you are actually guilty or accepted a plea deal, that was court. This is now and you will not make any progress if you dwell on what happened, or did not happen, in court.

When you think about what happened, and especially when you talk about what happened, use "I' all the time.

"I" knew she was 13 years old but "I" still had sex with her.

"I" knew she was high but "I" still had sex with her.

"I" held a knife to her throat and demanded she perform oral sex on me.

If you say something like she did not tell me her age, she came on to me, everyone knew she was easy, there was alcohol and drugs at the party, the way she was dressed everyone knew she was asking for it….all of those statements are excuses and attempts to minimize the situation and avoid accepting responsibility for YOUR actions.

You may have trouble at first being open about what you did. That is common! With practice you will get better at it. You will need to be able to tell your story to future employers, future significant others, and estranged friends and family members. Not everyone will understand or accept what you have done. That is ok. What you want them to hear is that you have not only acknowledged your responsibility for what happened, you have also taken corrective actions in your life to prevent it from ever happening again. You do not need to always go into a lot of detail about the circumstances and events. Sometimes, a simple and short but honest summary is sufficient.

There are numerous places in the Bible where God talks about confessing your sin and He will forgive you. It is absolutely true! Newsflash, He will forgive your sexual sins too! All of them. If you come to Him with a sincere heart that is truly sorrowful for what has happened, if you confess your sins to Him, He promises to forgive you. See Chapter 11 for more information.

Generally, people make good decisions and restrain from committing criminal actions. Things that should positively influence your decision-making may include family, friends, church attendance, daily Bible reading and prayer time, a spouse, police presence, or a code of ethics. When these influences are absent or ignored, a trigger (a temptation) has a better chance of negatively affecting your decision process.

You need to identify what the triggers were that lead to your decision(s) to commit a sex offense. There are more than likely several triggers that contributed to your poor decision(s). They are unique to you and you need to do some serious internal honest self-examination and figure out what they were.

Triggers could include things such as:
- Who you were living with and hanging out with
- What part of town you spending a lot of time in
- Gang membership or affiliation
- Anger management issues
- Drug or alcohol issues
- Mental health issues
- Pornography
- The internet and sex related websites

Once you have identified your triggers, you need to figure out what corrective actions you need to take to prevent them from becoming triggers ever again. For example if one of your triggers was the fact that you lived with other guys who routinely engaged in criminal activity and had little to no respect for women, then you clearly need to not allow yourself to be in such a situation ever again. In other words, find a different and healthier place to live! As another example, if your decision-making abilities were affected by drug or alcohol use, then you need to seek immediate and effective treatment to get clean and sober and stay that way. Likewise, if the internet is a problem, install software that blocks your ability to access websites that are not healthy for you.

Only you know what your triggers are and only you can take the actions needed to ensure they are not going to be problems again and lead you to making poor decisions that cause you to re-offend.

You may want to get into an accountability partnership with several others that you can trust and who will agree to not only challenge you periodically on your decision making but who will be there to support you and encourage you when you feel 'on the edge' of slipping and yielding to a trigger.

Questions to ask yourself:
1. Have I identified my triggers?

2. Am I honestly taking positive actions to manage my triggers?

3. Can I look in the mirror and tell my story using "I" and accepting responsibility for my actions?

4. Do I feel remorse for my actions?

5. Am I in compliance with the parole and probation requirements unique to my situation (such as therapy, classes, polygraphs, avoiding victims and specific areas, etc.)?

6. Am I in compliance with the registration unit's requirements?

7. Am I proactively taking questions and concerns to my Parole & Probation agent or raising them in group or individual counseling sessions?

8. Am I personally making smart decisions about how I think, act, and talk?

9. Am I personally making smart decisions about where I go when I leave the house?

10. Am I personally making smart decisions about who I see and talk to each day?

11. Am I personally making smart decisions about my use of the internet?

12. Do I have a trusted accountability partner?

13. Have I told my significant other all of the facts about me?

14. Am I going to church and rebuilding my spiritual foundation?

2 - Victim Perspective

While not all sex offenders have actual victims (e.g. Craigslist sting operations or undercover operations), most sex offenders fail to recognize that there are victims and victim's families involved. What you did, the crime you committed, created a victim. You may have traumatized that individual for life. What is done is done and cannot be undone. However, hearing from the victim's perspective can be sobering and insightful and may serve to help prevent you from reoffending.

Whether your victim was a stranger, a friend, or a family member, they are victims. Your actions were selfish and you clearly failed to take into account the feelings and reactions of the victim when you committed your offense. Whether that was intentional or just done out of ignorance, the result is the same: by your actions, you have made an innocent person a victim.

Some sobering questions for you to reflect on include:

- Did you consider the damage that you have done to the victim and how it would affect them for the rest of their life?

- When did your needs become so important that you could consciously decide to violate your victim?

- Did you consider the violation of trust and security that you have inflicted on the victim, especially if it was someone you knew?

Those are clearly some hard questions to answer but you need to spend some time giving the questions, and your answers, some thought. Most offenders are pretty clueless when it comes to the fact that they have created a victim and have traumatized them for life.

Understanding that and accepting that can be a helpful part of your determination not to re-offend.

Depending on your specific case, you may or may not be able to contact the victim directly or indirectly to apologize and express remorse for your actions. However, you can certainly go to God in prayer and confess your heart to Him and ask for His forgiveness and healing.

3 – Tips From Survivors

Here are several stories and survival tips from actual sex offenders. To protect their identities, names are not used nor are any geographically specific details included. These are provided to show you it is possible to overcome the stigma of being a sex offender and, with a faith-based approach, find a way to exist and have a semi-normal life again. There is hope!!

KEITH ROYS

A's story

He was arrested for a violent sex crime and served over 30 years in prison. He was recently released and is attending sex offender therapy classes. He has learned to accept responsibility for his actions and is able to clearly and honestly tell his story. He has a full time job and is an excellent worker. He also loves the Lord and thanks Him for sustaining him during his incarceration and guiding him in his healing through Bible studies and going to prison church. He has an apartment of his own and has his own car. He encourages you to be honest with prospective employers and emphasize your strengths and skills during interviews.

B's story

He was arrested for a non-violent sex crime against a minor who was a relative. He spent several years in prison and is now out on probation. He is living in a local shelter and is a recognized Christian leader there. His faith is strong and he teaches bible studies during the week to the other men in the shelter. He also preaches sermons about once a month. For him, rebuilding his spiritual foundation was essential for his healing. He now finds daily peace and strength through the Lord and is not shy about sharing it with others in need. He strongly encourages you to make God a part of your daily life. He also encourages you to look for part-time work anywhere you can find it. You do not need a full time regular job and doing part-time work will still pay the bills.

C's story

He was arrested for a sex crime and spent several years in prison. He is now out on probation and doing well. He has graduated from the therapy class and has passed his most recent polygraph. He is working as a self-employed handyman and has enhanced his skills and is confident in his abilities to tackle any remodeling project thrown his way. He loves the Lord and is grateful for His forgiveness and His love. He attends church regularly. He recently purchased a used vehicle of his own to use in his work.

D's story

He was arrested as part of a Craigslist sting operation involving detective's role playing minors. He served a couple years in prison and is out on probation. He has a safe place to live and a part time job with an employer who knows what happened and was willing to hire him and give him the opportunity to earn a paycheck. For him, confessing his sins and returning to his faith has been instrumental in his healing process. He got involved in the church inside prison and has continued to rebuild his spiritual foundation after his release. He has been in group therapy classes since his release and believes that they have been instrumental in getting him to identify his triggers and to accept responsibility for his decisions. He has several accountability partners that keep him focused. He has dated several women and has shared his story with each one on or before the third date. All have been accepting of his story and appreciated his upfront honesty. His advice is to you is to make God a part of your daily routine through reading devotionals and prayer time and to comply with all the rules and regulations.

<u>E's story</u>

She was arrested for a sex crime and served some time in prison. She is on probation and has graduated from sex offender therapy class. She learned how to share her story without fear of a negative response and the therapy classes were a big help for her. She has accepted responsibility for her actions and encourages you to do the same. The sooner you can, the sooner healing begins, and the sooner you can move on with your life she says.

KEITH ROYS

4 - Registration & Probation

As a sex offender, you most likely are required to register with the local police department. You will usually be required to register within 72 hours of your release. This is separate from the requirement to see your probation officer. Keep your probation officer informed of any issues you have with registration as well the status of your compliance with their requirements.

How often you need to see the registration unit depends on the severity of your crime. It may also be affected by your housing status; if you are homeless, you may be required to register weekly or more often. Usually you will be required to go to the registration unit at the police department on a monthly, quarterly, semi-annual, or annual basis. When you go, expect to be photographed. You will be asked to verify things such as your address, phone number, and employment information as well as any vehicles you drive, and any email addresses or social media identities you have (most offenders are not allowed to have social media accounts). Some agencies ask you to provide addresses that you spend more than five nights a month at other than your home address (for example, your girlfriend or your parent's house). All of this information is entered into the state and national database and is available on the public sex offender registry websites for your state and nationally.

KNOW YOUR NEXT REGISTRATION DATE! Failure to register within the time period required will result in an arrest warrant being issued. That will then cause your probation officer to take action, possibly violating you.

Most states do not allow sex offenders to be out wandering around on Halloween nor allow them to be home answering the door and handing out candy. Usually they require you to be at home, lights out, door closed, and a sign posted saying something like "NO CANDY". You can expect to get visited by the registration and or probation officers to verify you are at home and in compliance. Failure to be in compliance can result in serious consequences such as warrants and violations.

The registration unit may do random unannounced residence verifications. They can show up at any time and knock on your door to verify you actually live at the address you provided. If you are not home at the time, they usually leave a card or letter asking you to call them within 24 hours to verify you do live there.

There is no real way to get off the registry other than through the passing of time. If your charges are overturned or modified, it may be worth having an attorney review your case to see if a change in your registry status is warranted.

Some states have local groups that are trying to get the registry changed such as changing the access so that it is not publically available but only available for law enforcement use. One state court system has concluded that the website registration database is tantamount to public shaming. Other actions being considered include development of procedures to allow a registrant to earn his way off the registry, to minimize the amount of personal information displayed on the website, and to reduce the duration of the registration requirement to match the original felony crime penalty duration.

KEITH ROYS

5 - Travel

If you want to travel out of the state, you will need to coordinate with the registration unit. Their requirements may vary state to state, but usually they will want to know where you are going, for how long, and who you will be staying with. They will also usually ask you to call 24 hours prior to your departure and within 24 hours of your return. This is in addition to any requirements that your probation officer has for your travel.

Pay close attention to the registration requirements of the state you are traveling to as well. Some states require visiting sex offenders to register in that state if they are going to be in the state for more than 48 hours. Other states are less restrictive. Check with your registration unit or the state website where you are going. It is better to ask and be in compliance than to risk a violation.

International travel is a similar process. You will need to coordinate with your local registration unit and may be required to coordinate with the local law enforcement agency of the country you are visiting. Again, it is better to ask upfront and ensure you are in compliance than it is to risk a violation.

KEITH ROYS

6 - Public Perceptions

The fact that you are a sex offender can cause you to feel ashamed and afraid to interact with the public. You feel like everyone around you knows you are a sex offender and is judging you. The reality is that most people do not know your status and in most cases, those who do learn about your status are more interested in who you are now and not who you were then.

There will no doubt be those who are going to react negatively to your sex offender status. They may express disgust, anger, even hatred towards you. Your task is to remain calm and civil and get away from that person in any way possible as fast as possible. If you are being actively harassed, you need to contact the police for protection. Keep your probation officer informed as well as the registration unit.

Even though you are on the registry and even though your neighbors may see registration police stop by periodically, most people in your neighborhood are unaware of your status. That is not a license to act stupid or be disrespectful. It just means you should not walk around in fear or act paranoid. Be normal. Be polite. Be civil. The more friendly and normal you are the more people will not only accept you but if they find out about your status, they will balance that information with the person they have come to know. By in large, the public will accept you as long as you are not acting stupid. Do not hang out at strip clubs, hang out with drug or alcohol abusers, or run with the wrong crowd. Be the person who smiles, who says hello, who picks up the trash outside where you live, who holds the door open for ladies, and who is a good neighbor.

You will need to be aware of going to public places like the beach, the malls, the playgrounds, near schools, etc. You may have prohibitions from being around some places. It makes common sense to avoid places where your victim is at or where people like who you victimized hang out. Think about where you are going and how it would be perceived if your probation officer saw you or the registration unit saw you. Perceptions are important. It may be wise to take a trusted friend with you if you need to go someplace where someone could misinterpret your presence. You certainly should check with your probation officer or the registration unit if you have any questions or have some need to go to a location where it could be questioned why you are there.

7 - Jobs, Resumes, & Interview Tips

Getting a job as a convicted felon is challenging. Getting a job as a registered sex offender is even more challenging. For example, your conviction will prelude you from getting jobs where security clearances are required. Yet with patience, honesty, and perseverance, you can find employment. There are many major employers that will at least listen to your story during an interview. That is the time to not only be honest but to highlight all of your positive experiences, training, and skills.

When you prepare your resume, do not leave gaps for time served. Put in the facility name and location and list all of the training you completed, jobs you held, and skills you developed while inside. Be ready to provide copies of certificates and letters of reference.

Be prepared for rejection and closed doors. There are some employers who just refuse to hire felons and sex offenders. Shrug it off and keep applying. Stay positive.

Be smart about where you apply. For example, do not apply to schools or day care centers!

One basic ground rule is do not lie about your criminal history, your charges, or your parole and probation status. When filling out applications, some still have blanks for you to fill in regarding arrests, convictions, time served, etc. There are some initiatives in various states to remove those from the application. If the application you are filling out still asks it, fill it out in brief terms and put a note on it that says something to the effect of 'more information available during an interview'. You will still need to be honest during the interview and let them know about your background. Employers at some point will run a background check and it is better for them to validate what you have honestly told them than it is for them to find out that you have not been truthful and forthcoming about your background.

You do not necessarily need to go into explicit details about your charges and the events that led to your arrest unless your employer asks for the detailed information. Usually a simple but honest statement of facts is sufficient.

During the interview, you can say something like you made some poor decisions a few years ago and were arrested on these charges and served some time for them. Immediately move into a discussion of how your time served allowed you to identify your weaknesses, how you have taken positive corrective actions, how you have grown, and how you are in full compliance with all court ordered programs. Show them copies of courses and training you have completed, including your therapy graduation certificate. You may even be able to use your pastor or probation officer as a job reference.

KEITH ROYS

8 - Dating & Relationships

As a sex offender, it can be awkward trying to date someone. At what point do you reveal your background to them? You absolutely must do so if you intend to be intimate with them or have any sort of long term relationship with them.

Be smart in who you choose to date! For example, it would not be wise to date a woman with children if your offense was related to children. It also would not be wise to go to social functions (for example, birthday parties, bar-b-que's, movies, beach trips, etc.) with friends or family if children are going to be present or if your victim may be around.

The basic thumb rule is have 'the talk' with them on your third date, or sooner if you intend to be intimate with them. Be honest. Be open. As before, you do not necessarily need to go into explicit detail but you need to provide enough information so that they are informed and can decide whether to continue the relationship with you or back out. You should provide enough information so that if your probation officer contacts them, there are no surprises your probation officer will reveal to them that you have not already covered.

Some sex offenders have actually gotten married and not told their spouse anything about their status. Needless to say that is not wise. Some sex offenders sugar coat their background or downplay it to some simple criminal history and fail to identify the sex crime and registry aspects. Again, this does not usually go over well with a significant other if they learn after the fact that you withheld some information.

Most women are willing to accept you if you are humble, honest, upfront and open about your past. Explain it in simple terms and always follow up with how you have grown from the experience of serving time and being on probation and in therapy. Answer any questions honestly and let them decide whether to accept you and continue any form of relationship with you. If you have genuinely accepted responsibility for your actions and have moved forward with confidence and are doing well with employment and housing and compliance with court ordered programs and probation, that is viewed as being successful and most women will appreciate what you have gone through and are doing to move forward with your life.

Your friends and family deserve to know about your status especially if you intend to have any sort of interaction with them. As before, do not hide facts from them but also you do not provide explicit details unless asked and then only if you feel comfortable doing so and believe it will somehow help in healing or acceptance. Some friends will abandon you as will some family members. This may be permanent or temporary. Be patient and continue on with living your life. Your actions and your successes may eventually convince them over time to reestablish some sort of relationship with you.

KEITH ROYS

9 - Counseling and Treatment

It is fairly common for courts to order some form of treatment or therapy as part of your probation. The form and duration of this is usually determined by your probation officer.

In general there are two main types of therapy: group and individual. Depending on the nature of your crimes, you may be assigned to more than one type of therapy such as drug and alcohol treatment, domestic violence treatment, or anger management in addition to sex offender therapy.

The therapist and your probation officer will determine the initial frequency of meetings. It could be twice a week every week for a number of months. They will try to work with you and your work schedule if you are working but the bottom line is therapy is court-ordered and prevails over anything and everything else in your life. Failure to attend required sessions can result in disciplinary actions up to and including a finding of violation of probation and a return to prison.

There should be a phone number you can call if you cannot make a scheduled therapy session (e.g. you are sick or have an accident on the way to therapy). You absolutely also want to call your probation officer as soon as possible. Most therapists and probation officers are sympathetic to such situations, however if they become a habit, you can expect some adverse reactions.

In some cases, the therapist may recommend medical treatment such as medicine, injections, or other forms of therapy besides group or individual sessions.

Group sessions may have 15-25 people in attendance and they may include male and female sex offenders. Generally, you should expect to sign in before each session and be required to participate in each session. Check with the therapist or office staff for class rules but generally you are not allowed to bring cell phones or other music or recording devices into a session. You should not bring food or drink into a session. Make sure you use the bathroom before each session because you normally will not be able to leave the room once the session starts.

Session rules generally include no talking about what was said during the session outside of the session, respect each person who talks, raise your hand to talk, answer when you are asked a question, be respectful to the therapist and do not talk over or argue with them. If you have a problem with something that occurred during a session, talk it over with the therapist and your probation officer.

10 - Other Resources

The federal government maintains a national sex offender website through both the Department of Justice (https://www.nsopw.gov/en/Registry) and the Federal Bureau of Investigation (https://www.fbi.gov/scams-safety/registry). Links to each state sex offender website can be found through either of the federal websites. You can find good information about each state's registration requirements somewhere on the state registration webpage. This is useful when you are considering travel to another state or moving to another state. The federal website and most state websites have links to other useful information regarding resources, benefits, and support available to you.

Not all states have the same criminal code or definitions of what their sex crimes are. You will need to do some research to find out what the equivalent crime and registration requirements are for each state you want to visit or move to. In some cases, the registration requirements may be more severe and in other cases, less severe. For example, in your home state you may be required to register once every six months but in another state for the equivalent crime, they require you to register every 90 days. You can usually call or email the state registration unit for answers to specific questions.

KEITH ROYS

11 - Salvation

You may not fully realize it yet, but God loves you enough to provide you a way to find Him and gain His peace in your troubled life! He wants you to come to him, confess your sins, and accept His free gift of salvation and forgiveness! If you are not 100% certain of your salvation, read the following verses and pray a prayer like the one on the next page.

Ephesians 2:8-9 says that it is only by God's grace that you can be saved. There is nothing that you can do to earn it or work for it.

Romans 3:23 says all have sinned....that means you too! Sin has been in every person's life since Adam and Eve. Sin means we cannot be in God's holy presence.

Romans 6:23 says the penalty for sin is death...that means eternal separation from God and heaven.

Romans 5:8 says that even though we are condemned sinners, God loves us so much that He sent His son to pay our death penalty.

Romans 10:9 says that all you need to do is confess with your mouth that Jesus is Lord, that He died on the cross for your sins, and believe that God raised Him from death to life eternal.

Through what Jesus did on the cross, substituting His life for yours and dying on the cross in your place, His blood washes you clean of all of your sins and allows you once again to be in God's holy presence and guarantees you eternal life in heaven with Him!

If you believe this, pray something like this:
Lord God, I am a sinner. I believe you love me enough that what Jesus did on the cross paid my sin debt forever. Through His death and resurrection I now have life eternal in heaven and I thank You for that! Please forgive me of all of my sins and help me now to use my time to grow strong in Your word and share your love with others who need to hear it. Amen.

1 John 1:9 says that if we confess our sins, He will forgive and cleanse us! Accept that promise as truth and shed your burden of guilt and shame. Go forth with renewed confidence and build your foundation daily on His word!

Talk to a local pastor of a Bible preaching church to find out about worship service times and bible study classes.

Visit www.solidrock724.com to order additional resources or use the order form on the next page.

Order Form

Go to www.solidrock724.com for book descriptions. All books will be shipped from Amazon's Createspace publishing company. Send this order form along with a check or money order made out to Solid Rock Ministries to: Solid Rock Ministries, PO Box 38497, Baltimore, MD 21231. Please allow 2 to 3 weeks for shipping.

Book Title	Price	Quantity	Total
12 Weeks of Devotionals Vol 1	$12		
12 Weeks of Devotionals Vol 2	$12		
New Testament Survey*	$10		
12 Week Bible Study*	$10		
Bible Games and Activities	$10		
ABC's of Surviving Prison	$10		
Sex Offender Resource Guide	$12		
Shipping (per book)	**$2**		
		ORDER TOTAL:	

*Completion Certificate available on request

Send to:

Name:	
ID Number:	
Institution:	
Street Address:	
City:	
State:	
Zip:	
Gift from:	

KEITH ROYS

About the author

Keith Roys lives in Maryland where he works as the Operations Manager for his friend's electrical contracting company. He is working with several other Christian men and women to help improve the re-entry success of newly released inmates who seek to grow in Christ as they reintegrate into society and renew ties with family and friends.

Over his lifetime, he has met a number of people who, like himself, have been through some significant events in their lives. Some of these men and women found God for the first time during their time of crisis while others recognized that they had strayed from Him and, as prodigals, returned to the cross. After listening to their stories and praying with them, he felt led to write some materials to encourage them and to help them grow stronger in His Word.

To God be the glory!

www.ingramcontent.com/pod-product-compliance
Lightning Source LLC
Chambersburg PA
CBHW060651290526
45793CB00001B/494